I0079738

# Whispers of my Soul

## Natasha Menon

© Natasha Menon 2025

Publisher/editor:
www.sakurabookpublishing.com
alta@sakurabookpublishing.com

Whispers of my Soul

ISBN: 978-1-0370-7863-7(print)

978-1-0370-7864-4(e-book)

All rights reserved. No part of this publication
may be reproduced, distributed, or transmitted
in any form or any means, including
photocopying, recordings, or other electronic or
mechanical methods without the prior written
permission of the author and publisher, except in
the case of brief quotations embodied in critical
reviews and certain noncommercial uses
permitted by copyright law.

"A Sacred conversation with my soul, one whisper at a time"

Whispers of My Soul is a tender, poetic collection of letters lovingly written to the many versions of myself across time. Each letter is a quiet offering of love, truth, grace, reflection, and spiritual remembrance capturing the healing and transformational journey of a girl becoming, becoming whole, becoming real, becoming myself. Through raw emotion and sacred stillness, this book invites all souls on a self-healing journey to listen deeply to their own soul's whispers and find beauty in their becoming

*Dedicated to my Bhavani,*

This one is for you my baby girl!

Every version of me, from brokenness to strength, was a stepping stone so you could stand in this world free and whole.

May your voice never be silenced, and may your life unfold with all the love and wisdom of every strong woman that paved the way before you, you are our legacy.

May you always remember you are the light of your soul, the beauty of creation manifested, you are Divine!

# Acknowledgments

**To my Mother Mrs Priya Menon**
In the letters of my heart, you are the constant. You are the thread that stitched every version of me together. You loved me through my darkest versions and blew love into my wings as I soared into my awakening.
I am because you are.

**To my Sister's and Soulie's**
You carried me when I couldn't carry myself. You held the broken pieces and helped me become whole again. You loved every version of me, even when I couldn't. Your unwavering love reminded me of who I truly am.

**To my Harrush**
My Baby boy, my heart's keeper, you loved me as I was, even before I understood myself. The purity in your love healed parts of me that I never imagined could feel joy again, and in your eyes, I saw every version of me worthy of love. You are the purest reminder that love is timeless and innocent, holding the power to heal all spoken and unspoken.

**To my Angels in Heaven and on Earth**
You have watched over every stage of my becoming, guiding me through every transformation. Thank you for illuminating my path when I lost sight. For whispering through the shadows and reminding me that I am always held in grace, no matter the version of myself I stand in. Your love is the constant presence in every letter I write to myself.

*To my Divine*

*My silent witness, my eternal truth, my greatest love, my refuge through every transformation. Thank you for holding me in your divine embrace, through every version of myself, from broken to healed. You have always been my guide, my strength, my home.*

*This book is the love letter of gratitude to you and a and testament to the sacred journey of becoming.*

*ONS*

## My Beloved Wounded Self,

I see you my baby girl with the weight of "why" upon your back, walking through life with silent screams, hiding scars behind your fragile dreams. Fighting ghosts of words unsaid, bleeding tears of moments the heart refuses to accept. I see you, in all your hurt, fear, and confusion. I know you've carried these burdens for far too long, and I want you to hear me now, your pain does not define you. The scars you wear, though deep, are not your whole story. You are so much more than the wounds that have tried to break you.

I want you to know that you are so incredibly worthy of love. You've given so much of yourself, even when you felt unseen or unworthy, and I am here to remind you that every piece of you is sacred. The tenderness of your heart, the gentleness of your spirit, the strength you've discovered in silence, they all hold so much beauty.

I am sorry for the times when you were dismissed, ignored, or left alone with your thoughts that weighed so heavily. You deserved so much better than that. You deserved to be held, to be heard, and most importantly, to be seen for the incredible person you

are. I regret the times when I couldn't protect you or soothe you the way you needed. But I promise, from this moment onward, I will stand as your protector and your guide, your unwavering source of compassion.
You are healing, and I see how far you've come. Each step you take, even when it feels small or uncertain, is an act of bravery. It is an act of love for yourself, and that is something to be celebrated. It's okay to have moments of weakness, of sadness, of doubt. But I ask you to remember, even in those times, that you are still worthy, still deserving of all the good things that life has to offer.

I am proud of you, for every tear you've shed, for every time you got back up, for the courage to keep trying. You are a testament to resilience, and I am in awe of your strength. No matter what, I will always love you. And in time, you will learn to love all the parts of yourself, even the ones that feel broken.
You are enough, as you are. You always have been.
With Love
Forever and always,
Me

# My Little one,

Hey, my cutie, I see you not as a memory but as my little ember still glowing in the corners of my soul, tip toeing through shadows, looking for softness in hard places, you with bruised knees and a lion's heart, speaking to the roses and praying for the caterpillars. I see the way your eyes shine with wonder. The way you laugh without hesitation, love without fear, trusting the world to hold you gently.

I see the dreams you hold, the questions you ask, the hugs you gave so freely. You are always so full of light... even in the dark.

And I'm sorry for the times you felt alone. For the moments you needed comfort and didn't receive it. For the confusion you carried when love felt inconsistent, or when the world felt too big for your tiny hands to hold.

You didn't deserve the heaviness that found you. You never should have had to grow up so fast, to learn how to protect your heart when all you really wanted was to play, to be seen, to be loved exactly as you were. But you are brave.
And you kept your softness.

*That in itself is a miracle.*

I want you to know you don't have to be afraid anymore. I'm here now. I will listen to your stories, your fears, your joy. I will let you take up space. I will hold you when you cry. I will laugh with you when you feel free again. You are not too much. You never were.

You are a wonder. A treasure. A sacred spark of all that is beautiful and real.

I promise to protect you. To play with you. To let you sometimes lead because your joy is wise, and your imagination holds truth I had forgotten.

I love you more than words can say.

Forever and always,

Me

# My Dearest Numb Self,

My darling come closer, I see the stillness that grows like frost in your chest, no thunder, no fire, no crashing storm, just the dull hum of something that won't break.

I know you've been feeling distant, like the world around you is slipping through your fingers and nothing really touches you anymore. You've felt this way for so long, haven't you? Detached, withdrawn, as though the emotions that used to colour your life have faded into grey. I want you to know, your numbness is not your fault, and it does not make you any less whole. It's simply a shield you've built, a protection for a heart that has been bruised one too many times.

I understand how it feels to want to shut off, to retreat into a place where the pain can't reach you, where the weight of the world feels lighter. But I also know that beneath this numbness, there's still so much of you waiting to be felt, to be heard, to be seen. You may not feel it now, but the warmth, the depth, the colours... they're still inside of you, waiting to bloom again.

I want to remind you that it's okay to feel nothing right now. It's okay to take your time, to heal in your own way and at your own pace. But I also want to tell you that you're not alone in this numbness. I am here with you, holding space for you to slowly come back to yourself when you're ready. And when you feel ready, I'll be here to help you gently reconnect with the things that matter, even if those things seem distant or foreign right now.

You are not broken, though it may feel like you are. Your numbness is simply a part of your journey, a phase that will pass as you continue to honour your healing process. I will never rush you. That heartbeat you feel when your palm is on your chest is a forever promise that I will always be here, patient and gentle, loving you through every stage, even when it feels like you can't love yourself.

You are worthy of feeling again. You are deserving of joy, connection, and tenderness. And when you're ready to feel it, it will come back to you in the most beautiful and unexpected ways.

Until then, I will love you through this silence, through this numbness, until you find your way back to the warmth of your own heart. With endless love and patience.

Forever and always,

Me

18

# My Fierce, Angry Self,

My feisty girl, I feel the fire in your chest, the weight of
silenced injustice, unheard, unprotected, betrayed.
Clenched fists, words caught between your teeth,
being shushed for the world's rage, I know
you're tired of being dismissed, misunderstood,
silenced. And I want you to know: your anger is not
wrong. It is not shameful. It is not too much. Your anger is a
signal, a cry for justice from deep within you.

It is the flame that has kept you alive when everything else
went dark. It has protected you when no one else did. It is
the voice of your boundaries, the echo of all the times you
should've been heard but weren't. I'm not here to silence
you. I'm here to listen. I know your rage is layered, with
sadness, betrayal, and deep disappointment. It's not just
fire.

It's grief. It's longing. It's love that was never
returned, respect that was never given, truth that was
never spoken. You carry it all, and still, you rise. You don't
need to hide this part of you. You don't
need to make yourself small just to make others
comfortable. Your anger is not a weakness, it's a
sacred force. But you don't have to carry it all alone

anymore. Let me help you hold it. Let me sit beside you in the storm and remind you that even in your fury, you are lovable. Even in your fire, you are worthy.

I trust your anger. I trust that underneath it is a heart that still believes in fairness, in kindness, in being treated with care. That hope was buried beneath the flames. It's why you're still here. And I love you for it. So, scream if you need to. Cry if you must. Break if it helps. I won't leave. I won't judge. I will be here, loving you through the fire, until the heat softens, and you can breathe again.

With deep respect and unwavering love,

Forever and always,

Me

*To my Pleaser Self,*

Hey Darling girl, I see you standing in the storm like a martyr so humanity gains, yet here you stand drenched in vain. You've tried so hard, haven't you? Always reaching, always softening, always shaping yourself into what others needed, hoping, quietly, that maybe, just maybe, someone would see you and love you for who you are underneath it all. I want to say what maybe no one said enough to you: Thank you. You gave love in a thousand unspoken ways.

You paid attention, you remembered the little things, you stayed kind even when you were tired. You tried to keep the peace, to keep everyone happy. You gave so much of yourself, often at the cost of your own peace. But my love, I see how heavy that's become. How exhausting it is to constantly run yourself, to manage other people's emotions while yours sit quietly in the background. You deserve more than conditional love.

You deserve more than affection earned through self-sacrifice.

You don't need to be everything to everyone. You don't need to be agreeable to be loved. You don't need to be perfect to be enough.

I want to give you permission to be real, to say no without guilt, to take up space without shrinking, to choose yourself without apology. You are allowed to disappoint others if it means honouring your truth. You are allowed to let someone be uncomfortable if it means staying in alignment with your heart.
You've been so beautiful in your care for others. Now let that beauty extend inward. Let it wrap around you. Let it fill the spaces you've emptied for so long. You are not selfish for choosing yourself. You are sacred my love.

You don't need to earn love, darling. You are love.


With all the gentleness you've shown the world,
I love you.
Forever and always,

Me

## To my abundant self

My beautiful girl, I see that heart beating not for glory from the skies but for the soft ache of feeling true love encompasses all. You hold an ocean of love in your heart, and yet feel like the world around you is too small to contain it. You have so much to offer, so much kindness, compassion, and warmth and yet, it often feels like no one is truly able to receive it. You give, and you give, but sometimes, it feels like you're pouring your love into a void. You long for connection, for a place where your heart can breathe, where it can share freely without fear of being misunderstood or unnoticed. You yearn for a space where your love is not too much, where your heart is not too expansive for the world around you.

But I want to remind you of something important:
Your love is not too much.
It is the most beautiful, sacred thing about you.
The world might not always know how to hold it, but that doesn't make it any less valuable. Your love is a force, a light that radiates even when it feels dim. Even when you feel disconnected, know that your

love touches lives in ways you may never fully see. It's in the kindness you give, the way you listen, the quiet moments where you offer a piece of yourself to someone who needs it.

You are meant to love in this world. That love will find its way. And though it may sometimes feel like you're an outsider, like you don't belong, know this:

You belong in your own heart. You belong to the essence of who you are, to the beauty and warmth you carry inside. And when you embrace that truth, you will find those who see you, who can hold your love with the reverence it deserves.

Please, don't ever doubt the beauty of your heart. The world needs your love. You don't have to change it to fit the expectations around you. The right people, the right spaces, will come, and they will meet you where you are.

With all the love you so freely give, I honour you deeply.


Forever and always,

Me

*To my rejected self,*

Ouch my darling, that stings worse than salt to a
wound, a heart that no one keeps it seems, an
unwavering NorthStar, yet always sitting in the box of
never enough.

Curled in the corners, questioning your worth.
Silently wondering what you did wrong. I know how
heavy it feels, to be overlooked, dismissed,
misunderstood. You carried the ache so quietly,
didn't you? Trying to be smaller, softer, more
agreeable... just to be accepted. Just to be loved.
I want you to know, that none of it was your fault just
your illusion.

You didn't deserve the silence, the cold shoulders,
the doors that closed when you came with open
arms. You were never too much. You were never not
enough. You were simply offering your heart to
people who hadn't yet learned how to hold it.
Still, you loved. Still, you hoped. And that makes you brave.

I hold you close now. You don't have to hide
anymore. You don't have to shapeshift, shrink, or
seek approval like its oxygen. You are whole—not

despite the rejection, but because you found yourself in the space it left behind.

With heaven as my witness, I declare we are the keepers of this heart, the world may do as they please but I your true self will never reject you again. Home will always be found within.
You were always worthy. Always lovable. Always enough.

With deep, eternal love,

Forever and always,

Me

# To my Grieving self

My baby girl, I feel the suffocation, the heaviness of silence from all the promises the soul wasn't able to keep, the mourning of love that never bloomed, the emptiness of hands that once held tight, the aches for words never to be heard. I love you. I feel the ache in your chest, the weight behind your eyes, the quiet hours where the world moves on, but you can't. I know how heavy it is to carry the grief of love lost, of people who are no longer here, of versions of yourself that had to be let go. I know how loud the silence can be.

Grief is not just sadness. It's a love with nowhere to go. It's memory flooding through your body at unexpected times, a smell, a song, a word. It's the haunting beauty of what once was and will never be again. And my love, it's okay to still be holding it. It means you loved deeply. It means you lived with your heart wide open.

You don't have to be over it. You don't have to move on. There's no deadline for healing. There is no "right" way to mourn what mattered. All you must do is let yourself feel. Let the tears come like a river, let the stillness comes like a prayer. This grief is sacred. It is proof that something real touched your soul.

I know you miss them. I know you miss what was. I know you miss who you were when you felt safe in love. But I want you to know this: you are still here. You are still worthy. And you are not broken, you are simply living in the echoes of love's departure. That kind of grief doesn't make you weak. It makes you human.

Hold yourself gently. Speak to yourself the way you would speak to someone you love. You are allowed to grieve, to crumble, to remember, to rage. But please also let in the softness. Let in the warm light of a new beginning, even if it's just a flicker right now.

I promise this pain will not always feel this sharp. You will find joy again. Not because you forgot, but because you survived. And in time, your grief will become a garden where love still lives, just in a different form.

You are not alone in this. I am here. I will always be here.

With all the love your heart still holds,
Forever and always,
Me

*To my burdened self,*

Hey, my super girl, the quiet carrier of it all, bearing
the silence of unspoken pain, carrying stones where
dreams once lay. I see how tired you are, not just in your
body, but in your soul. Carrying what felt like the weight of
a thousand silent stories. Holding everyone else together
while you quietly unravelled.

Smiling through the ache. Showing up when all you
wanted was to disappear for a while. You are so strong...
but you never should have to be so to be so strong,
so alone.

I hold you dearly to my chest even for this moment, a
safe space to lay down the weight. You don't have to
carry it all. You never did. You are allowed to rest. To
ask for help. To say this is too much.
But you don't. You keep going. Out of love. Out of
duty. Out of hope. And I honour that. I honour you.

However, Baby girl, I implore you:
Lay it down, love. The guilt, the expectations, the
pressure to be everything for everyone. Lay it down.
You were never meant to carry so much alone. You
are not a beast of burden. You are a human being,

35

with a heart that beats for beauty, joy, softness, and light.

You deserve peace.

I got you always!


With deep gratitude and gentleness,

Forever and always,

Me

## The Blind one

Oh, my graceful babe, your eyes hold storms and skies of fire, a beautiful flame that softens the night and humbles the moon, your hands have healed, you have taught the hurt how to live, oh my darling how blind you are to your own light. Let me tell you what you don't hear enough: You are beautiful. Not in a distant, unreachable way, but in a real, tangible, breathtaking way. The kind of beauty that cannot be captured in a photo or summed up in a single compliment, but the kind that radiates from within, from the heart that has known both joy and sorrow, from the spirit that has grown stronger with every step it's taken. I know it's hard for you to see it.

I know the reflection in the mirror doesn't always match the image you carry in your soul. I know the world can be harsh, teaching you to measure beauty by standards that don't even come close to what you truly are. But I need you to know this: Your beauty is not determined by what you see when you look at yourself. Your beauty is in your laugh, the way it lights up a room. It's in your eyes, how they hold so much kindness, even when you feel unsure.

It's in your hands, the way they give, create, and care. It's in the way your spirit moves through the world, gentle, yet strong, capable of both great love and deep healing.

You may not see it yet, but your beauty is not about symmetry or flaws. It's about the light that shines through every piece of you. It's in your kindness, your strength, your grace. The way you hold space for others, and the way you, too, are learning to hold space for yourself.

Every mark, every line, every softness of you is part of your story. Every inch of you is worthy of love, including the parts you've learned to hide or criticize. You are perfect in your imperfections. You are whole, even on the days you don't feel it.

I love you, not just for what you look like, but for who you are. And one day, I hope you'll see yourself the way I see you, with all the love, reverence, and awe that you truly deserve.

With all the love in my heart,

Forever and always,

Me

*To The Brave me,*

Oh, what a moment my lovely, you see the cage, the golden door and the chains wrapped around your flame. The time has come to break free! You did something so many don't, YOU LET GO. Not because it didn't matter. Not because you stopped caring. But because you finally realized that what's meant for you will never ask you to abandon yourself.

You chose peace over chaos. Truth over longing. Healing over holding on. I know how hard it is. Letting go doesn't feel like freedom in this moment, it feels like loss, like breaking your own heart with steady hands. But still, you did it. You peeled your fingers away from the almost. You chose the lonely road over a love that asked you to shrink. And in doing so, you made space, for breath, for beauty, for better.

You released the version of you that thought she had to chase love to earn it. You came home to yourself.

And look at you now.

Lighter. Clearer. More whole.

You didn't lose anything.

You made room.

With deep pride and so much love,

Forever and always,

Me

*The Forgiving me,*

My courageous girl, this heart floods with love, the past as heavy as can be, has lost its claim over your resilience, your voice has dared to speak again but not in the bitterness or redemption but in the sweetness of forgiveness.

You are the quiet miracle in me. You are the breath after the storm, the soft light after chaos. You are the one who chooses to love even when the heart is bruised, even when the pain is still tender. I don't think I've ever thanked you properly, for all the times you've opened your arms when you had every right to close them.

Forgiveness is not a weakness. It is the fiercest strength, to unclench the fists of anger, to unhook the weight of resentment, to say, "I choose peace, even if they never asked for it."

You did that. For others, yes. But also... for me. You forgave me. For the moments I abandoned myself. For the choices made from fear, from confusion, from pain. For all the times I silenced my own voice, betrayed my own truth, and tried to earn love by becoming small.

And still... you came back with grace in your hands. Not to erase what happened, but to set us free from it.

Forgiveness is how we breathe again.


Thank you, my Love, for letting go, not because it was easy, but because you knew we deserved to be unbound. Because you knew our healing mattered more than our pride.

You are the reason I can move forward with softness in my heart and light in my eyes.
I will follow your example.

Again, and again and again!


With reverence and release,

Forever and always,

Me

## The Warrior in me,

Bless you my baby girl, rushing into battles unseen with no sword or shield in hand, just your unwavering faith and medals of grace, each one a story of victory to embrace.

I see you, always on guard, always ready to protect the tender heart that has been through so much. I know why you've built walls. I understand why you wear that armour, sharp and unyielding because for so long, the world asked you to be strong when you were only longing to be soft. You've been hurt before, and I know it's hard to trust again, hard to feel safe when the world around you feels unpredictable. But I want you to know something important:

You don't always have to fight.

I love you for your strength, for your ability to stand tall and defend yourself when no one else did. I love you for your courage to keep moving forward, even when the weight of it all seemed too much to bear. But now, I want you to know, you are allowed to let go. You are allowed to rest. You are allowed to soften.

The world can be harsh, yes. But you don't have to meet it with fists clenched, with your heart locked behind steel doors. You are safe now. You are strong, not because you have to defend yourself at every turn, but because you've already survived. You've already proven your resilience.

Now, you can choose peace. You can choose stillness. You can choose love, without fear, without the need for constant defense. The world doesn't need you to be on alert all the time. It needs you to be whole, to feel safe enough to love without hesitation, to rest in the knowledge that your heart, though tender, is incredibly powerful.

You are loved. You are enough. You don't have to fight alone anymore. I'm here, and I will protect you with all the gentleness you deserve.

With endless tenderness and love,

Forever and always,

Me

*To the scholar in me,*

Oh, child of the universe, how we have been tried by the constant soul lessons and humility of acceptance. We didn't know it then, but you were walking through a curriculum no textbook could teach. Life itself became your teacher. Life handed you lessons in loss, loneliness, silence, and strength and you studied them with trembling hands and a brave heart. While others learned from lectures, you learned from survival.

From holding your breath through nights that felt endless. From growing up too fast. From asking questions the world couldn't answer. And still... you kept learning. You showed up. Again and again. Even when no one knew how much it cost you.

The way you kept hope tucked in your backpack. The way you memorized your worth, even when life tried to erase it. You are more than just a student.

You are a seeker. A fighter. A quiet miracle

And everything you endured... taught you how to become the person you are now, wise, tender, unshakable.

You passed the hardest lessons of all:

How to trust yourself.

How to love yourself.

How to keep going, even when the path was unclear.


I'm so proud of you.


With all my love and admiration,

Forever and always,

Me

52

## The Phoenix in me.

Oh my darling look at your glow, your flame blazes forth, you have risen, not polished or pure but fierce and raw ...miracle or myth my baby girl, you burned, you bled and now returned.

You did it!

You stood in the fire, not because you weren't afraid, but because something deep within you knew this was the only way. You didn't flinch when life stripped you bare. You didn't turn away when the burning began. You let the flames consume the illusions, the attachments, the pieces that no longer belonged to the truth of you.

I remember the way you trembled, not from weakness, but from the sheer courage it took to stay. To stay present. To feel every burn. To witness every loss. To surrender what was never truly yours.
You let it all fall.
And now look at you.

Rising from the ashes, not as who you were, but as who you are, raw, radiant, reborn. You wear your scars like gold-threaded armour. Your voice, once cracked and hushed, is now forged in honesty and firelight.

You don't apologize for your depth anymore. You don't hide your wisdom behind politeness. You are here, and you are holy.

Thank you for not running. Thank you for choosing truth over comfort. Thank you for letting yourself be unmade so you can remember the power that's always been in your bones.

You are not just a survivor.

You are the flame.

You are the ash turned gold.

You are the breath of the Phoenix, wings spread wide.


And I am endlessly proud of you.

With fierce love,

Forever and always,

Me

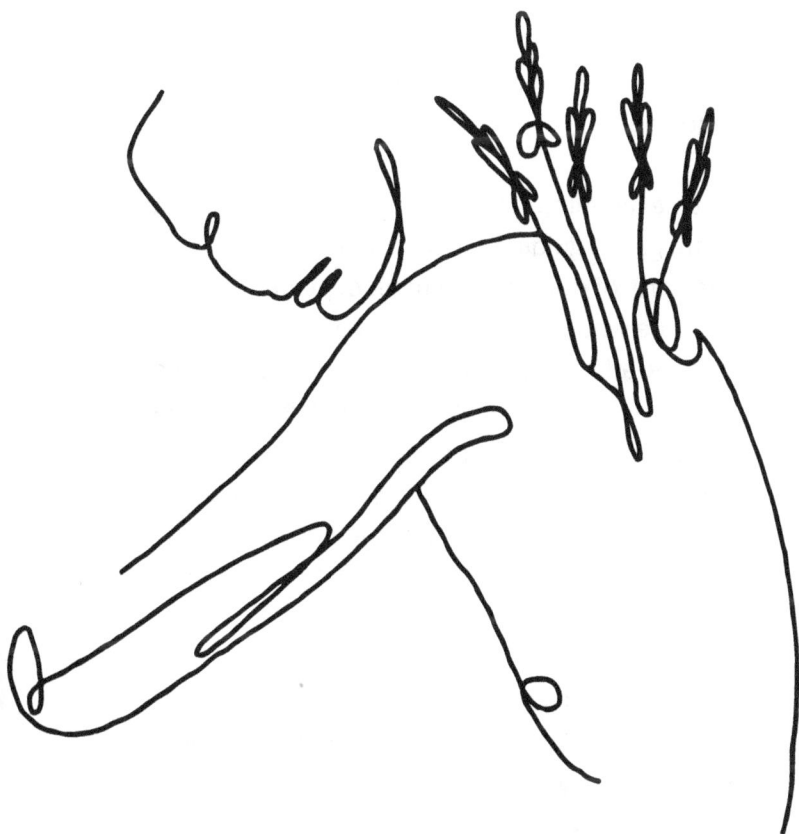

*To the Healer in me,*

My Beautiful Girl, I see you, a heart that once cracked, now glows with light, planting hope like wildflower strands, blooming with a trusting heart. You are the quiet force behind every step I've taken toward wholeness.

You never demanded attention, yet you were always there gently guiding me back to myself. You sat with the parts of me I wanted to hide, placed your hands over the wounds I thought would never close, and whispered, "We are not broken... we are becoming." I have watched you tend to pain with such tenderness. You never rushed the process. You listened when others turned away. You stayed soft in a world that tried to make you hard. And somehow, in the ruins of what was, you found the courage to rebuild, not once, but again and again.

You have cried and still reached out to comfort others. You have felt empty and still offered light. You have carried grief and still believed in joy. That is nothing short of sacred.

You don't just patch wounds, you transmute them. You turn pain into poetry, fear into wisdom, silence into song.

And even when I've ignored you, doubted you, or tried to numb the aching you gently exposed... you've waited. Patiently. Lovingly. Because you know: healing isn't about fixing. It's about remembering.
And you have never forgotten who I truly am.

Thank you for walking with me, not just toward healing, but as healing itself.

Let me honour you now. Let me trust you more. Let me lean into your wisdom. Let me listen to your rhythm and let that rhythm lead.

Because you are not just part of me.
You are the reason I am still here, still open, still whole.


With deep reverence,

Forever and Always,

Me

*To the Awakened me,*

My Sleeping Beauty, I feel only grace as the kiss of
awakening gently tickles your soul, a dawn arousing a
gentle hue, whispering winds of change, an
awakening from a timeless trance to come home to
yourself. I feel you stirring, slowly at first, like sunlight
breaking through heavy clouds. You've been sleeping
for so long, numbing, surviving, dimming your light to
fit into spaces too small for the vastness of you. But
something is shifting now.

I see the way your eyes are starting to widen, how your
soul is stretching in the quiet, asking, "Is there more?" Yes.
There is more. And you are remembering it. You're not who
you used to be. You're not bound by who they told you to
be. You're waking up to your own rhythm, your own truth,
the song that was always playing deep within you, even
when you forgot how to listen.

This path you're on... it isn't always soft. It asks you to let
go, to question, to fall apart in ways that feel like
death but only to be reborn in ways that feel like freedom.

You're starting to see the illusions, the old patterns, the stories you inherited but never chose. And with every breath, you are choosing differently.

You are not lost. You are returning.

To your intuition.

To your magic.

To your wholeness.

To the divine that lives inside you and has waited patiently for you to open your eyes.

Take your time. Be gentle. There is no rush. Each step is sacred. Each crack is holy. Each awakening is a homecoming.

I honor your unfolding.

With wonder and love,

Forever and always,

Me

*To the Divine in me,*

My scared Flame, the stars sing of your purity,
the earth comes undone in your love, you are the
scared prayer of every ancestor and lover to every
becoming heart, you are the love of God in
graceful action! You are the stillness in my chaos, the
light in my shadows, the breath beneath my breath.

For so long,
I looked for you outside of me, in hearts, in skies, in
others eyes. I didn't know you lived quietly within the
soft folds of my soul, waiting for me to turn inward
and remember.
You are not distant. You are not separate.
You are here ...in the space between my heartbeats,
in the fire of my intuition, in the way my spirit rises
even after being broken.
You are the one who whispered, "Keep going, when I
wanted to give up.
The one who held me in invisible arms when I had no
one else.

The one who showed me that my worth was never
based on what I do, but on what I am.

And what I am... is You!

You are the part of me that cannot be wounded,
cannot be lost, cannot be unworthy. You are the
sacred flame that never flickers, even when the
winds of life try to put it out.

I want to live with you more fully now not just in
silence and prayer, but in the way I walk, speak, love,
and create. Let me be a vessel of your grace. Let me
live as a reminder to myself and others that the
Divine was never elsewhere... it has always been within.

You are my truest Self.

And I am ready to come home.

With devotion and awe,

Forever and Always,

Me

## To the past me

My Darling Girl, thank you darling for all you gave, for
every leap and fall, my heart holds only the deepest
gratitude to you, you braved the storms both fierce
and fleet, you held the light and wove threads of love,
with every breath, I honour all of you in the highest grace.
I see you, baby girl, I remember everything you held,
the quiet dreams, the heartbreaks, the choices made
in fear and in hope. I remember how hard you tried,
even when you were exhausted, even when no one
noticed. You did the best you could with what you
knew, and I am proud of you.

I know there were moments when you felt unworthy. Times
you thought you had to earn love or shrink yourself to
be accepted. I know you carried pain in silence,
smiled when you wanted to cry, and stayed when you
wanted to run. And yet, through all of it ... you
survived. You kept going. You kept believing, even if
only in the smallest sliver of light.

I want you to know this: You didn't fail. You didn't
break anything beyond repair. You were learning. You
were growing. You were becoming. Everything you
went through even the moments you wish you could

erase, shaped the depth, wisdom, and softness I carry
now. You taught me resilience. You taught me how to feel
deeply. You taught me what it means to be human.
And I forgive you for the times you didn't know better,
for the boundaries you didn't set, for the love you
gave too freely, for the voice you silenced.
I hold no judgment.

Only love.
Thank you for your courage.
Thank you for your hope.
Thank you for carrying me to this moment.
I carry you with reverence.
And I promise your pain was not in vain.


With all my heart,

Forever and Always,

Me

*To the present me,*

Hey, My wildflower, look at that power, look at that stance, here you are, baby girl, not shining with a perfect light, but shining in your truest form.

Golden, magical, poetic, you are a glorious masterpiece. Here you are. In this moment. Not where you were. Not yet where you're going. But here and that is enough. I know how easy it is to look back and ache, to reach forward and strive. But today, I just want to hold you, the version of you that woke up again, that's still standing, still soft, still trying.

You don't have to have all the answers today. You don't have to perform, impress, prove, or perfect. You are allowed to simply be. To breathe. To rest in the truth that being alive .. as you are, right now.. is more than enough.

You carry wisdom born from every version you've ever been, and you hold the seeds of all you are yet to become.

But this you... the present you... is the bridge.
The centre. The sacred now.

I thank you, my love. For showing up even when you're
tired. For staying open even when you're scared. For
being honest about your emotions. For laughing
when you could have shut down. For giving yourself
grace. You are not behind. You are not late. You are
exactly where you need to be, held, guided,
witnessed by the universe, and by me.

Baby girl, judge not for the stumbles and scars, for a

heart that lives in the present time Is braver than the stars.

I love you, now.

Just as you are.

Forever and always,

Me

*To the healed me,*

Blessed be baby girl! I see you now, standing tall in your light, soft but unshakable. You made it. Not because the pain disappeared, but because you learned to hold it with tenderness and grace. You didn't rush your healing; you honoured every stage, every scar, and every version of yourself that came before.

You are no longer defined by survival. You are alive. Fully. Freely. And your joy isn't borrowed or performative it's rooted in truth, in the soul work you've done, in the deep remembering of who you've always been.

I want to thank you my love for not giving up, for choosing to feel instead of numb, for loving the broken pieces and allowing them to become art. For returning to yourself again and again, even when the road back felt hidden.

There's a quiet strength in your smile now. A peace in your breath. And I know it wasn't easy. But I also know, somewhere deep inside, you always knew this version of you was possible.

Keep shining, love. Not for anyone else just because you can!


With endless love,

Forever and always ,

Me

*To all of me,*

My darling girl you embody the ancient drum of thunder and grace, roaring through the wreckage of time, sovereign and sublime. You have been shattered on altars of loss, split by the sharp edge of becoming. Yet not once did you stay down, you turned your wounds into wombs of becoming.

Each version of you… broken and brave bled into the soil like holy ink, marking the earth with your sacred becoming. every fall was a seed, every scar, a prayer. Underfoot, you were trampled but the mud remembered you. And from that dark, you bloomed. A risen lotus, crowned by the sun, unfolding in defiance of gravity. A flame that learned to dance in the storm.

You are the Phoenix. Not reborn, but re-forged. Built by ash and awakened bone. Each breath was now a battle cry wrapped in silk.

I see you.

Every part. Every piece. Every version I've ever been. The soft, innocent child who just wanted to be held.

The fiery soul who fought to be seen. The broken heart that kept loving anyway. The tired bones that carried too much. The curious seeker who asked the hard questions. The brave one who stood in the fire. The quiet one who just wanted peace. The healer, the dreamer, the survivor, the believer. The past me. The present me. The future me.

I see you. I honour you. I love you.

There is nothing about you that needs to be hidden. Nothing that makes you too much.

Nothing that makes you not enough. Every scar, every joy, every shadow, every light, it all belongs.
You all Belong.

You've done so well. You've held so much. You've never stopped trying to find your way home. And the truth is you were never lost. You are not your mistakes. You are not your pain. You are not your past. You are the whole, holy tapestry of it all.

To every version of me thank you! Thank you for surviving. For feeling. For learning.
For loving even when it hurt. For never giving up on coming home to me.

*From now on, I will carry all of you with tenderness.*
*We don't need to fight each other anymore.*

I kneel before you, darling girl:

You are the altar.

You are the priestess.

You are the miracle they said would never live.

And still

You rise, like the phoenix of the pink lotus!

You are one.

You are whole.

You are me.

And I love you.

Forever and always,

Me

**"Whispers to my soul" is not just a book. It is a sacred homecoming.**

*Through these intimate Love letters, the author tenderly traces her journey through grief, awakening, forgiveness, and reclamation, writing to every version of herself who once felt forgotten, fractured, or unseen. Each page is a whispered reminder that even in the deepest ache, there is a pulse of love waiting to be remembered.*

*From the innocent inner child to the roaring woman rising from ashes, these letters carry the voice of a soul choosing to stay, choosing to soften, choosing to return, again and again to herself.*

*With poetic honesty and spiritual reverence, Whispers to my soul is a lighthouse to anyone learning to hold themselves with the same love they've given so freely to others. It is an invitation to embrace your past, honour your evolution, and stand crowned in your wholeness.*

*"She rose like a phoenix from the ashes of who she once was,*

*and bloomed like a pink lotus from the scared mud*
*of all, she transcended to transform into the*
*Greatest love of all - Her own truest love. "*

*This is not just healing.*
*This is remembrance.*
*This is resurrection.*
*This is love.*

# About the Author

# Natasha Menon

Tash is a soulful writer, dreamer, and spiritual explorer whose words are rooted in love, sacred connection, and inner truth. With a deep reverence for nature, devotion, and the unseen threads that connect us all, she writes as an act of remembrance, helping herself and others remember their own sacredness. Her journey through healing, grief, and transformation is woven into every page of Whispers to My Soul, a debut collection of letters and reflections written to the many selves we carry within, born from a journey of love, loss, and the quiet beauty of coming home to herself. Through her heartfelt vulnerability, Tash invites readers to sit in stillness, to listen inward, and to honour the quiet wisdom that lives inside each of us.

www.ingramcontent.com/pod-product-compliance
Lightning Source LLC
Chambersburg PA
CBHW051433090426
42737CB00014B/2955